What

know about

PRAYER

... but were afraid to ask

What you always wanted to know about

PRAYER

... but were afraid to ask

IAN COFFEY

Unless otherwise indicated, all Scripture references are from the Holy
Bible: New International Version (NIV), copyright © 1973, 1978, 1984
by the International Bible Society.
Other versions are marked:
Message: Scripture taken from *The Message*. Copyright © 1993,
1994, 1995, 1996, 2000, 2001, 2002. Used by permission of NavPress
Publishing Group.
Street: Rob Lacey, *The Street Bible* (Grand Rapids, Michigan: Zondervan,
2003).
Concept development, editing, design and production by CWR
Cover image: sxc.hu
Printed in Finland by WS Bookwell
ISBN: 978-1-85345-415-8

For Alec, Lyndon, Graham, Clive and Nick
with gratitude for our years together as a prayer group.

CONTENTS

INTRODUCTION

Questions are good for you.

They can make you think, help you connect with people, push your boundaries and become stepping-stones to knowledge and understanding.

But questions can sometimes be bad for you.

They can gnaw at your confidence, corrode your courage, destroy your trust and become roadblocks to faith.

But questions exist and somehow we have to deal with them.

When I am on the internet and visiting a website I often click on the Frequently Asked Questions button – the FAQ button – as it offers a short cut and saves scrolling through pages of information. It deals with the questions most people ask on a subject and offers answers that are (hopefully) clear and concise.

This book – *What you always wanted to know about PRAYER ... but were afraid to ask* – offers answers to some FAQs on the topic of prayer. It is not a detailed theological or philosophical exploration of the mystery of prayer or a manual of the different ways in which we can experience and enjoy this amazing gift of God. Others more gifted than me have written about these things. This is – forgive me – a basic dummy's guide to prayer. It looks at seven FAQs about prayer and offers some answers.

Two groups of people had a share in the writing and I want to acknowledge their help. Mutley Baptist Church in Plymouth, England was our home for twelve happy years before, in 2004, I was called as Senior Pastor to Crossroads Church in Geneva. Both Christian communities are full of wonderful people with questions about prayer. The process of leading, caring, teaching and encouraging them has shaped this book.

And many of them, through the gentle persistence of their faith, have inspired me to learn more about prayer.

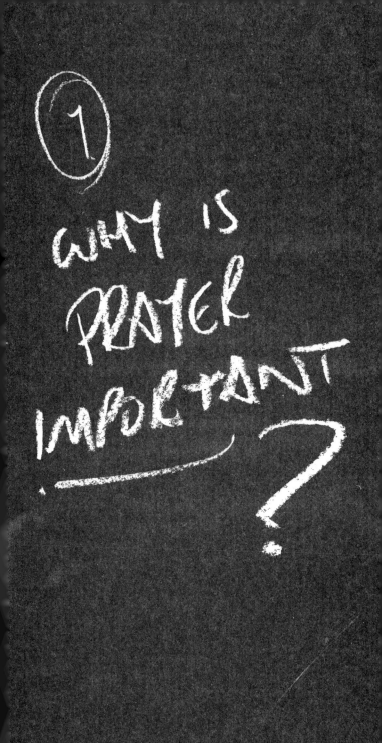

1. WHY IS PRAYER IMPORTANT?

There are many aspiring sportsmen and women who would like to bend a ball like Beckham, drop kick like Jonny Wilkinson or run a marathon as fast as Paula Radcliffe. And the lesson they will learn along the way is that to be that good takes a lot of practice.

There is a story told about Paderewski, the Polish pianist and composer, whose hours of practice were legendary. He played before a delighted Queen Victoria who greeted his performance with the words: 'Mr Paderewski, you are a genius!' He modestly responded, 'Perhaps, your majesty, but before that I was a drudge!'

What is true in the natural world applies in the spiritual realm, too; to become accomplished at anything takes time, skill and practice. Prayer is an important part of a healthy spiritual life. Anyone who displays a rich spirituality will say that prayer plays a vital role.

The fact that many of us find prayer difficult reveals how important it is.

Prayer by its simplest definition means having a conversation with God. Most of us don't find conversation difficult because we do it all the time. Research has shown that on average a man uses 2,000 words a day, whilst a woman employs 7,000 – which explains why women, generally speaking, are better at forming and developing relationships than men. Words are important building-blocks of communication.

But prayer is more than talking to God, it also involves cultivating the ability to listen as He speaks to us – it is a two-way street. And the more effort we put into it, the greater the reward that follows.

It is about growing in our relationship with God and discovering more of His purpose for our lives. This is how one writer describes the part that prayer plays in this:

> Prayer is the conversation of friends. It is not a mere convenience for letting God know what we are thinking or what we want. Prayer is that for which we were made. It is at the heart of God's plan of salvation. To understand the tremendous privilege and import of prayer we need to see it in the context of God's purpose to have a relationship with his people.[1]

THE FIRST BIG PRAYER IN THE BIBLE

Genesis is the first book in the Bible and is all about beginnings. We read the account of creation and the Fall, and then on to the stage of history steps Abraham, who became known as the friend of God. In the middle of the Genesis story of Abraham and God's dealings with him there is a record of the first full-scale prayer recorded in the Bible (see Gen. 18:20–33).

Abraham and his wife Sarah were old and childless – but God promised that an heir would be born to them in their old age. At this point in the story, God set a date for the promise to be fulfilled within twelve months. The announcement was made by the Lord in a personal visit to Abraham at his tent in Mamre. (See Gen. 18:1. This is what is known as a *theophony* – an appearance of the Lord Jesus before His birth on earth as a baby in Bethlehem. The other two visitors were angels; compare 18:16 with 19:1.)

At the end of the meeting the Lord decided to take Abraham into His confidence and reveal what He was about to do. There were two cities close to where Abraham lived – Sodom and Gomorrah – and they were infamous. God announced to Abraham His intention to see for Himself the truth or otherwise of their reputation for evil. The two angels were sent as heavenly emissaries while Abraham and the Lord engaged in earnest conversation.

What follows next in the Bible is an account that, at first reading, appears confusing and strange. Abraham asks God if He will really destroy the two cities if, say, fifty righteous people can be found there. He poses the question based on his understanding that God in His very character is upright and true: 'Will not the Judge of all the earth do right?' (Gen. 18:25). If this is the case, how could God lump the righteous in with the wicked and leave them both to the same fate?

This dialogue continues with Abraham whittling away in his debate with God, reducing the number of righteous people who might be found in the cities; from forty-five down to the final figure of ten, Abraham bargains back and forth on no less than six occasions. Sounding like a Middle-Eastern market trader, Abraham negotiates the Lord down to the bottom-line figure of ten righteous people. The deal is done; if just ten are found the cities will be spared the impending judgment.

> Is God to be bartered with?

This conversation poses two immediate problems. First, we are uncomfortable with the idea of a God who judges people. Our modern Western minds are conditioned to think of a kind God who loves everyone so much that He could never be cross with them. Second, the thought of Abraham bargaining with God seems foreign to our ears. Is God to be bartered with? Is prayer nothing more than some spiritual negotiation ploy with a reluctant deity? Can judgment be bought off?

15

We misunderstand Scripture by hastily reaching such conclusions. The Bible talks equally of God's righteous standards and His redeeming grace. Reading about the state of affairs in Sodom and Gomorrah, it is obvious that the last shreds of human decency had been stripped away and anarchy ruled. Genesis 19 gives a graphic account of the total breakdown of the rule of law in the two cities.

When we read of Abraham pleading with God for the cities to be spared for the sake of ten righteous people it is important to recall who initiated the conversation in the first place. Abraham didn't stumble upon God's plan – it was graciously revealed to him. This whole incident was a part of God's training for Abraham as a man of faith and the father of those who would be children of faith. God was drawing Abraham in close to His heart.

WHAT DO WE LEARN ABOUT THE IMPORTANCE OF PRAYER?

Abraham's lesson in faith teaches us two truths about prayer and explains why it is so important in developing a healthy spiritual life.

It is based on our relationship with God

God revealed His intentions to Abraham because of his place in His overall purposes. Abraham would become the father of all those who believe (see Rom. 4:11), and as such needed to understand that the promise of a child was bound up within a bigger plan. Abraham's 'blessing' was not something merely personal but something through which God would touch the world. Abraham would be blessed – but in turn he would be a blessing. Genesis 12:1–3 records God's original promise to Abraham when He called him to leave his home comforts and securities.

The pathway to that blessing lay in Abraham's obedience to God's call. At various points in his story Abraham's obedience was tested as his faith was refined.

The Sodom and Gomorrah incident must be read in the light of God's training programme for Abraham's life. He is nurturing in him a concern for others – a concern that is evidenced by standing in the place of others and interceding on their behalf. This is described as the first intercessory prayer in the Bible because it shows Abraham interceding for a city facing judgment and pleading for God's mercy for the sake of a few righteous people.

Here is God letting Abraham in on His plans, including him in His programme and training him in His ways.

As one writer has expressed it:

> As with Abraham, so with us, God wants to develop this personal relationship for the benefit of others. We are never the end of the line. He has other people he wants us to direct into his ways, for we each have unique circles of contact and influence. We should not see prayer as a duty, one of the ingredients of the Christian package which we have to accept. Rather, prayer is the means by which our living contact with God is deepened and enriched, and because we love him we want to know him better, to be more effective for him in the world, to count for God here and now. All that happens as we pray for other people.[2]

It is based on our partnership with God

We can indulge in many philosophical questions about prayer. Here are a few for starters:

- If God has already decided what to do, then what is the point of praying?

- How can prayer change the mind of an all-powerful, all-knowing God?
- If prayer can change God's mind – then what sort of God are we dealing with in the first place?
- Isn't prayer simply a release for our inner emotions and desires – more a personal comfort blanket than an actual force for change?

Strange as it may seem to our ears, the Bible instructs us that God has chosen to involve us in His plans. A crucial key to understanding how prayer works is bound up in the single word *partnership*.

> God has chosen to involve us in His plans

The very prayers we pray are inspired by God Himself; it is He who plants the seeds of prayer in our hearts. Romans 8:26–7 speaks of the Holy Spirit of God inspiring and directing our prayers. Abraham's intercession led to the deliverance of his nephew Lot from the destruction that fell on Sodom and Gomorrah, and the postscript that is recorded declares: '… God … remembered Abraham …' (Gen. 19:29).

When we were small, perhaps we took delight in volunteering to help Mum in the kitchen or Dad in the garden. How often must our parents or guardians have thought it would be quicker and easier to tackle the job without our youthful enthusiasm!

But what of those occasions when we heard them say, 'I really need your help today'? How many of us learned to do what we do now with skill because a parent or another adult took time to be with us?

When we ask the question: 'Why is prayer important?' two answers stare us in the face from the pages of

Scripture. One is that God wants us to grow in our relationship with Him and the second is that in His love and grace He calls us to be partners with Him by becoming involved in His world.

As staggering as it may seem, we have a part to play in God's unfolding purpose for the world.

And prayer is the door by which we enter.

NOTES
1. Tim Chester, *The Message of Prayer, The Bible Speaks Today – Bible Themes Series* (Leicester: IVP, 2003) p.27. Used with permission.
2. David Jackman, *Abraham – Believing God in an alien world* (Leicester: IVP, 1987) pp.123–4.

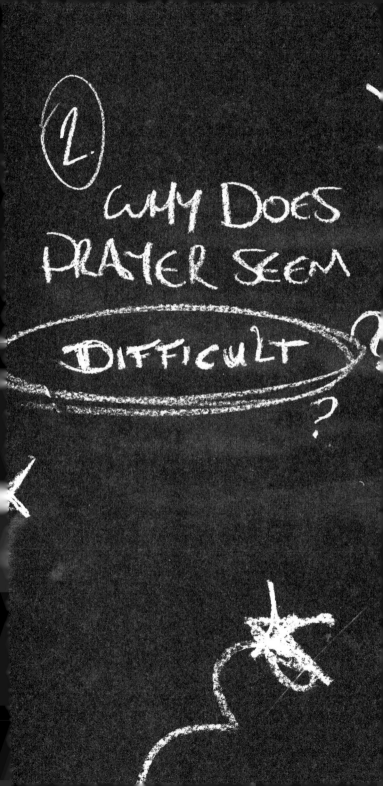

2.

WHY DOES
PRAYER SEEM
DIFFICULT?

2. WHY DOES PRAYER SEEM DIFFICULT?

One of my sons came home after his first week at school and announced he would not be going back. Anxious to find out what had upset him, my wife and I asked why he had reached such a firm decision. 'Well,' he announced with a hostile glare, 'you've been telling me for ages that when I went to school I'd be able to read books by myself. I've been there a whole week and I still can't read!'

I have a hunch that sums up some of our feelings of failure when it comes to prayer. We feel we have been followers of Christ long enough to become proficient at it – yet so often we fall short. As a result we decide to quit trying altogether.

Why does prayer seem difficult?

JESUS TASTED DISAPPOINTMENT

Being let down by close friends is an uncomfortable experience. Jesus faced that on the evening He was arrested and Matthew, in his Gospel, paints a vivid account of what took place (see 26:31–56).

Jesus had shared a special meal with His disciples in a borrowed room and then the group left to make the short journey to a hill just outside Jerusalem called the Mount of Olives. In a garden grove filled with olive trees, Jesus spoke to His close friends in the final minutes before His arrest. The garden was called Gethsemane, which is a name based on an Aramaic word for an oil press. It was a place Jesus and His followers visited frequently. Some have seen a strong parallel between the name of the garden and the agonising experience the Lord Jesus underwent there. An oil press is 'a place of crushing' and that is what Jesus experienced. Others point out the link between the first Adam's failure and defeat in a garden (Eden) and the second Adam's (ie Jesus') triumph and victory. (See how the other three Gospels add bits of information to complete the picture of this climactic event: Mark 14:32ff, Luke 22:39ff and John 18:1ff.)

From Matthew's notes of the conversation we learn that Jesus predicts that the disciples are about to abandon Him, but reassures them that in spite of what is to take place (He is referring to His trial and crucifixion) He will rise again and meet them back in Galilee. True to form, Peter is the first to speak and pledges his unswerving loyalty come what may. Jesus prophesies that before the dawn chorus Peter will break that promise no less than three times. Peter dismisses this, and the other disciples follow him in declaring their solidarity.

Jesus then takes the inner circle of disciples – Peter, James and John – to one side and shares His deep sense of disturbance. He invites them to sit and pray with Him in this dark hour. Jesus faces the darkness by turning to His Father in deep impassioned prayer, but His loyal friends fall fast asleep.

Prayer ... is essential if we are to resist evil ...

We don't know for sure how long Jesus spent in prayer that night but we are told that on three occasions He came to His disciples and found them fast asleep. As He faced the most difficult hours of His earthly life, the Lord Jesus prayed alone.

The first time Jesus found His disciples asleep He made a comment which Peter, James and John remembered so clearly that it was carefully recorded: 'Watch and pray so that you will not fall into temptation. The spirit is willing, but the body is weak' (Matt. 26:41).

Although Jesus tasted disappointment that night in Gethsemane He was not disillusioned because, as this verse reveals, He both knew and understood what makes people tick. But contained in this verse is a word of warning coupled with a word of instruction. Jesus is saying both to His friends in the garden olive grove and to His followers in every age and place that prayer may be difficult but it is essential if we are to resist evil and stay clean.

The colourful paraphrase of *The Message* hammers the point home:

> 'Stay alert; be in prayer so you don't wander into temptation without even knowing you're in danger. There is a part of you that is eager, ready for anything in God. But there's another part that's as lazy as an old dog sleeping by the fire.' (Matt. 26:41)

A BATTLE ON THREE FRONTS

A follower of Christ has to face a battle that is fought on three fronts – the world, the flesh and the devil – and all three conspire against anyone who gets serious about prayer.

Each of them exerts a powerful pull against the desire to pray.

The world
This is the organised system of human life that ignores God and sets itself up in opposition to His rule. Its very essence is self-sufficiency with human pride at its core. Prayer, in that environment, is like a fish out of water.

Prayer is based on our need for God; worldliness dictates that we have no such need.

We are called to live in the world yet not to be of it and we are commanded to love people yet not fall in love with the world's standards and desires (see 1 John 2:15–17). One unknown writer put it well:

The ship's place is in the sea,
But God pity the ship when the sea gets into it.
The Christian's place is in the world, but God pity the Christian if the world gets the best of them.

Everything that worldliness represents pushes us away from the need to pray.

The flesh

When Jesus said to His three close friends that their spirits were willing but their bodies weak, He was referring to the weakness of our human nature. The Greek word for 'flesh' is used and implies our nature that is tainted and damaged by sin.

On this second front we have to fight the constant battle between prayer and our fallen human nature, which don't get on together. Our fallen nature says, 'Take it easy, feed your appetites, look after number one.'

That is why the disciples fell asleep at Jesus' critical hour of need. They wanted to help – but their personal interest in some restful 'shut-eye' came first.

Part of the reason we struggle to pray is that it goes against our human nature – and that is a strong force to reckon with.

> Prayer is based on our need for God; worldliness dictates that we have no such need

The devil

Forget the cartoon caricature of the ugly man in a red boiler suit carrying a pitchfork – he loves people to be taken in by that PR stunt. Evil has a personality behind it and Paul, the Christian leader, made no apology for explaining the nature of the fight. This is not a human enemy that can be tackled with the weapons of conventional warfare. Those who follow Christ are ranged against evil powers and spiritual forces that have a commander at their helm (see Eph. 6:12).

These forces recognise the power that comes through prayer. As an old couplet by William Cowper expresses it: 'Satan trembles when he sees/The weakest saint upon their knees.'

Part of the reason we struggle to pray is that there are powerful forces determined that as few as possible should access these mighty weapons of mass destruction.

FALLING FOR THE LIES

It is little wonder that prayer is a struggle at times when we consider the forces ranged against us. Perhaps – like me – you are amazed that any one of us prays at all! But that just underlines how great God's grace is in being able to give people a desire to worship and pray.

This three-fronted battlefield sees some major assaults against those who want to pray. There is also the more subtle propaganda war that drip-feeds our minds with negative messages. These messages are designed to push prayer to the back of our minds and the bottom of our agendas. Here are just a few:

It's too difficult

But to be good at anything takes time and practice,

and the rewards and blessings of prayer are so great it is worth all the effort. As we said earlier, the David Beckhams, Jonny Wilkinsons and Paula Radcliffes of this world remind us that there is no gain without pain. 'Little prayer equals little power' is an abiding principle of the spiritual life. But 'Through prayer comes power' is the equation's exciting opposite.

Prayer is boring

Many things that are important are boring in the sense that they involve hard work. Routine can become tedious and that is why we need constantly to be challenged and stimulated. Many find praying with another person or a small group a great help. Prayer in itself isn't boring, but the way we go about it may need a fresh approach from time to time.

Prayer attracts weird people

The unspoken part of this objection is: '… and I don't want to end up like them!'

This statement is not totally true. The vast majority of those who pray are happy, holy, normal people. In my experience they are people who live very fulfilled lives characterised by serving others. It is true that prayer ministry does attract some who are slightly eccentric – but they would be eccentric anyway. It is not prayer that has produced the eccentricity – what matters is that they have a desire to communicate with God and discover His heart. This piece of propaganda doesn't stand up to the light of real experience.

It's a specialist gift that I don't have

It is true that some people are called to a specialist ministry of prayer – but that doesn't let the rest of us off the hook. Not all have the New Testament gifting of evangelism (bringing good news) – but all Christians are called to bear witness to Christ. In the same way, some may have a calling to a life dedicated to prayer, but no follower of Jesus is exempted from the call to pray.

I'm more of a do-er than a pray-er

I have lost count of the times people have told me 'I'm more of a Martha than a Mary'. This comment is based on Luke 10:38–42 where Jesus visited the home of two friends who were sisters. Mary sat and listened to Jesus teaching while Martha busied herself with the hospitality arrangements. Some people see the two sisters as examples of the activist (Martha) and the more reflective (Mary) types of personality. Of course we are all different in temperament and personality and we shall see in the next chapter how these differences show up in our approach to prayer. But the very point of the story is that whatever type of person we are, we need to make room for Jesus.

> 'I'm more of a Martha than a Mary'

Martha – the activist – is told to take a leaf out of Mary's book. The practice of prayer is vital for us all – not just for some.

TRY THE 5 X 7 CHALLENGE

The answer to the question, 'How do you eat an elephant?' is well known. The answer is, 'In bite-sized pieces.'

You may feel your prayer life needs to improve by miles – but why not start with a few inches?

The 5 x 7 challenge invites you to make a pledge to pray

five minutes more for the next seven days. Perhaps you already pray every day – well, add five minutes to the routine. Some of us struggle to pray at all, so the challenge for us will be to start out. You can do it anywhere and anytime – but over the next week give an extra thirty-five minutes of your time over to God.

You may ask, 'What do I pray for?' Well, if you're stuck try using a newspaper, as there are plenty of people who need our prayers. Pray for your neighbours, friends and family, pray for your community and your local church.

And where is the challenge? Ask the Lord Jesus Christ to teach you how to pray – and see what happens. Have a look at some of the testimonies in the 'P.S.' section at the end of this book to find out what others have discovered about prayer.

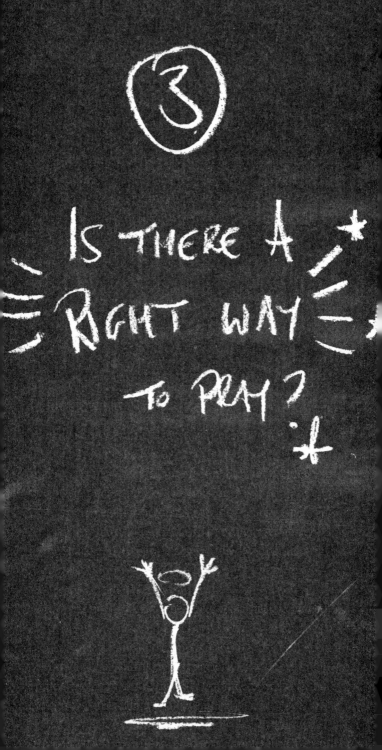

3. IS THERE A RIGHT WAY TO PRAY?

One of the most famous prayers in the world is the one Jesus taught His disciples. Here are the familiar words of the Lord's Prayer from the author of *The Street Bible*, by Rob Lacey. In this remarkable book it appears under the heading 'Template for Talking to God':

> God in heaven, you're our Dad.
> We respect everything you stand for. We want others to.
> Please bring heaven on earth: people living life your way, like the angels do.
> Please bring us what we need to keep us going each day.
> Please acquit us, as we cancel our grievances and throw them all away.
> Please pull us back from the edge of evil, if we're falling, or being thrown.
> 'Cos you're all that really matters; you're able to do it and you're to take the credit.
> You're on your own.
> It's your throne.
> Absolutely!
> (*Street*, p.300)

These words remind us that Jesus wanted His disciples to learn that prayer was about everyday language and images. They are particularly helpful as we consider our third FAQ about prayer: *Is there a right way to pray?*

SCARED OF TRIPPING OVER

I heard once of a man who, while attending a business conference, was summoned to be introduced to the distinguished guest of honour due to speak to the delegates. The man was carrying his mid-morning coffee as he was led across the room and introduced by name to the honoured celebrity. Flushed with embarrassment, the executive missed the short step, overbalanced and flung his coffee over the immaculately attired guest.

It is the stuff of all our nightmares – getting it wrong on an important occasion and never living down the shame.

We face inhibitions when it comes to prayer, and such a lack of confidence can paralyse our good intentions. Am I doing it the right way? Should I sit, kneel, stand or walk about when I pray? What am I meant to do with my hands – and is it right to bow my head? And which language does God prefer: Shakespeare or Lacey, King James or *The Message*, English or tongues? Or are the rumours true – God only speaks Yiddish?!

THE GIFT OF UNIQUENESS

Take a look at your hands for a moment. Do you realise that no two human fingerprints are the same? Fingerprints offer an infallible means of identification. Other personal characteristics change, but fingerprints do not.

We are each unique and special to God

Just as no two people have identical fingerprints, so no two spiritual experiences are the same. We are each unique and special to God, and understanding that stupendous fact is one of the most liberating discoveries we can ever make. Realising this truth releases us to pray.

One of the best books I have read on prayer was

written by a Spanish psychiatrist, Pablo Martinez. He explains how temperament, personality and experience affect the way we pray. Being introvert or extrovert determines the style of praying we like, and our physiological functions play their part as well. There are four predominant types:

- Thinking type (driven by logic)
- Feeling type (driven by feelings)
- Intuitive type (looking beyond what is)
- Sensation type (driven by the senses)

Each type possesses strengths and weaknesses and favours particular approaches to prayer. When the types are mixed they enrich each other, producing prayer synergy. Martinez concludes:

> Jesus, the perfect man, held all four functions in perfect balance. He has been the only human being to hold them in harmony ... it is reassuring to reach the conclusion that temperament is the seal that stamps our individual uniqueness in our relationship with God.[1]

BE YOURSELF IN CHRIST

Prayer is expressed through our personality – the very 'youness' of you is special to God. That is not an excuse for laziness or permission to remain unchanged. The very word 'disciple' implies one who learns, changes and grows. But we are set free in Christ to be ourselves and not conform to anyone else's mould. Pablo Martinez offers this perceptive quote:

> If I do not want what you want, please try not to tell me

that my want is wrong.

Or if I believe other than you, at least pause before you correct my view.

Or if my emotion is less than yours or more – given the same circumstances – try not to ask me to feel more strongly or weakly.

Or yet if I act, or fail to act, in the manner of your design for action, let me be.

I do not, for the moment at least, ask you to understand me.

That will come only when you are willing to give up changing me into a copy of you.[2]

PRAYER ACCORDING TO JESUS

Jesus taught about prayer – and He practised it too. From His teaching, preserved in the Gospels, we learn some important principles that help us in developing our prayer lives.[3]

In His famous Sermon on the Mount teaching on prayer, Jesus warns about several pitfalls and puts forward a famous pattern (see Matt. 6:5–15).

He pinpoints three pitfalls that are as relevant today as they were then. Pride, superstition and unforgiveness are always lurking around when people get serious about prayer.

Pride

The religious leaders of Jesus' day loved to be seen praying because it showed (so they thought) what spiritual people they were. Jesus burst the bubble of their hypocrisy by announcing that they had been paid in full. If prayer simply plays for public recognition, that's all it will get!

The story is recorded of a minister invited to open

an important building, who prayed: 'O Lord, let this gathering be fired by the motto of our church: *Nec tamen consumebatur*, which as thou knowest, O Lord, is Latin for "and yet it was not consumed" …'[4]

By contrast, Jesus tells those who are serious about prayer to find a quiet place and seek God privately. The word translated 'room' is the Greek word *tamion* and conveys the idea of a cupboard or larder, which suggests getting away from everyone. Prayer is not meant to be a public performance, but an act of private devotion.

> Jesus burst the bubble of their hypocrisy

This does not mean, however, that there is no place for prayer meetings or even large gatherings to pray. The point that Jesus makes is to do with the audience we address when we pray.

Superstition

Jesus highlights the pitfall of seeing prayer as a kind of magic incantation. When He speaks of 'babbling like pagans' (Matt. 6:7) it brings to mind people who have learned a prayer by heart and repeat it over and over without any sense of trust or meaning. The Greek word that is used, *battologeo*, means 'to repeat idly'. It carries the idea of a prayer that is repeated mechanically, devoid of any heart or reality.

These are empty words from an empty heart, offered in a superstitious hope that all will be well. Picture the football player running onto the pitch and crossing himself, or the person who repeats a prayer as a formula to win the lottery, and you will catch the drift.

Jesus is not condemning persistent prayer where we repeatedly bring a request to God. He is challenging empty superstition that has no faith attached to it.

Unforgiveness

According to Jesus this is not so much a pitfall as a colossal roadblock. 'If we do not forgive we will not be forgiven' is one of the clearest statements we will ever hear on prayer (see Matt. 6:14–15). And in case we are in any doubt, a well-known parable is devoted to the topic (see Matt. 18:25–35).

A servant is let off an enormous debt and then bullies a friend to repay a trifling loan.

It is a story of scandalous double standards: a man who was glad to receive grace with open arms but refused to dispense the same in return. Our prayers will not travel far if they are shackled by resentment and unforgiveness.

The famous pattern that Jesus taught in the Sermon on the Mount has become known as the Lord's Prayer. Translated into hundreds of languages and used for two thousand years, it has become a uniting point for the Christian family across the world.

... with the Lord's Prayer ... my blurred mind finds focus

It is a prayer in its own right and many, myself included, use it in their daily prayers. I confess there are times when my prayers are hard going and my mind is confused with many things. But with the Lord's Prayer I know my sometimes wandering thoughts are harnessed and my blurred mind finds focus.

The prayer also offers a pattern for all our prayers. The prayer can be broken down into seven short phrases, three directly dealing with God and four describing our own needs.

The first three phrases remind us:

- That our relationship is with a heavenly Father
- That we approach Him with honour and respect
- That our prime focus is His kingly rule.

The final four statements deal with:

- Our daily physical needs
- Our need to be forgiven and forgiving
- Our need to pursue purity
- Our need to find power to overcome evil.

This is a helpful template to guide our prayers and deliver us from the babbling that Jesus warned about.

Three men were in a boat that was sinking. The situation was serious and all they could do was pray. The first man said he wouldn't because he was unsure of his beliefs. The second said he couldn't because he didn't know any suitable prayers for sinking boats. The third prayed: 'Lord, we are in a mess. Please get us out of this and we will never trouble you for anything again.'

Is there a right way to pray? The simple answer is – from the heart. David, the psalmist, did just that:

Hear, O LORD, and answer me,
for I am poor and needy.
Guard my life, for I am devoted to you.
You are my God; save your servant
who trusts in you.
Have mercy on me, O Lord,
for I call to you all day long.
Bring joy to your servant,
for to you, O Lord,
I lift up my soul.

You are forgiving and good, O Lord,
abounding in love to all who call to you.
Hear my prayer, O LORD;
listen to my cry for mercy.
In the day of my trouble I will call to you,
for you will answer me.
(Psa. 86:1–7)

NOTES

1. Pablo Martinez, *Prayer Life – How personality affects the way you pray*
(Carlisle: Spring Harvest Publishing Division and Paternoster Lifestyle,
2002) p.34. Used with permission. See also Chapters 1–3 that deal with the
psychology of prayer.

2. Op. cit., Martinez, p.35. From D. Keirsey and M. Bates, *Please Understand
Me* (Del Mar, California: Prometheus Nemesis Books, 1978) p.1. Used with
permission.

3. Professor James Dunn highlights four key themes in Jesus' teaching on
prayer: (1) trust, (2) forgiveness, (3) persistence and (4) community. See
J. Green and S. McKnight, (eds) *Dictionary of Jesus and the Gospel* (Illinois:
IVP, 1992), pp.617–625.

4. E.M. Baliklock, *Our Lord's Teaching on Prayer* (London: Oliphants Ltd,
1964) p.16.

4. WHY ARE SOME PRAYERS UNANSWERED?

The woman was desperately anxious. She had brought her son up with Christian values and an understanding of her faith. She had prayed for him faithfully through his growing years but he showed little interest in the gospel. Like his father, he was content to lead his own life with no room for God. He enjoyed what others call 'the good life', fathered a son with a girl he lived with, and now he was planning to move abroad. His mother remained convinced that if he made the move then he would lose the only Christian influence in his life – herself.

She decided to spend the night in prayer in a small chapel and – with many tears – she wrestled through the night claiming the promises of God. She firmly believed that God could stop her son carrying out his plan to move abroad. Imagine her devastation when morning came and she discovered that he had gone, even as she prayed.

Here was one Christian left to handle a personal dilemma many of us have faced – why are some of our prayers unanswered?

APPEARING DRUNK AND DISORDERLY

It is never comfortable to be misunderstood and even worse to be wrongly accused of something. There is a story in the Bible of a woman in desperate need who was mistaken for being drunk when, in fact, she was pouring her heart out to God in prayer.

The story of Hannah (found in 1 Samuel 1–2) begins with great sadness and ends in overwhelming joy. She was one of two wives of a man named Elkanah who lived in the hill country of Ephraim. Their family situation was filled with tension: Hannah was not able to conceive, but Elkanah's second wife – Peninnah – had several children and went out of her way to parade her 'success'. This was a source of friction between the two women for years but became sharper at some of the religious festivals they attended as a family.

They would travel annually to the tabernacle based in Shiloh and, having shared in worship, they would sit for a family feast where portions of the sacrificial meat would be shared. Peninnah was surrounded by her sons and daughters while Hannah sat alone. Although Elkanah's heart went out to Hannah and he sought to comfort her, she came to dread these family occasions because Peninnah used every opportunity to provoke her to the point where she was desperately upset and unable to eat. According to Exodus 23:14–17, this trip to Shiloh would have occurred as many as three times a year for various festivals. But it seems that Elkanah's family made this an annual event (see 1 Sam. 2:19). It involved the whole family undertaking a thirty-mile round trip spread over several days. These big family occasions became a source of great unhappiness to Hannah. There was no element of celebration for her – they simply underlined her disappointment.

> ... she had been pouring out her heart to God ...

One night things came to a head: the family was going to bed but Hannah knew she wouldn't sleep. She made her way back to the tabernacle where there was only an elderly priest left on duty. Hannah fell to her knees and wept her prayer to God. She had prayed about this issue many, many times over the years and even now her words didn't come out right – she was mixed up with sorrow, pain, anger and guilt. But she made a serious promise. If God answered her prayer and gave her the son she longed for, she in turn would offer him back to serve the Lord Yahweh for all his days.

The elderly priest, Eli, kept a close eye on this woman who chose to pray long after closing time. Her demeanour suggested that it was not the Holy Spirit she was interested in but a different kind of spirit altogether! He rebuked Hannah for being drunk in a place of prayer and got ready to throw her out. But when she pointed out her desperation and the fact that she had been pouring out her heart to God, Eli felt rebuked and challenged. This was not someone abusing the place of prayer but, rather, seeking God with all she had.

Hannah left, not with a rebuke but a blessing as Eli sent her on her way in peace. Miraculously, that peace surrounded her and carried her forward for many days until – in the course of time, God's time – Hannah had the joy of holding in her arms a living, breathing answer to her prayer. Two things are important to note from this passage. First (1 Sam. 1:18), although there was no immediate answer there was a turning point in Hannah's life. She began to eat and her outlook changed. Second (v.20), the phrase 'in the course of time' suggests it was not an instantaneous answer but that she had to wait in patient faith.

Little wonder she called her son Samuel, which sounds like the Hebrew for 'heard of God'.

LESSONS THROUGH A LONELY LADY

The Bible records Hannah's heart-rending story for a reason. God could have simply said, 'And, behold, Samuel was born and became a mighty leader in Israel'

– instead we have Hannah's story, which gives us hope. The following New Testament comment tells us about the rich value of the Old Testament: 'For everything that was written in the past was written to teach us, so that through endurance and the encouragement of the Scriptures we might have hope' (Rom. 15:4). Here are some pearls from Hannah's pain:

- **Desperate prayers are not unusual**
  Heaven is used to 999 calls and we should not be afraid to make them.
- **Prayer is often the last resort – when it should be the first**
  Hannah had nowhere else to go. The sooner we run out of options the quicker we get down to serious praying.
- **Sharing a burden lessens the load**
  Eli became the listening ear that Hannah so desperately needed, but to find it she needed to express her vulnerability.
- **We can find rest – even though there is no quick answer**
  The narrative records that this distressing incident brought Hannah to a place of peace even though her immediate problem was not solved.
- **God can do the impossible**
  Hannah's story has a happy ending – but not all our stories end with our getting what we ask for. Yet the circumstances surrounding Samuel's birth remind us that God can do impossible things when He chooses. However hard we find it to accept, we are left with the conclusion that when we don't get what we pray for, it has to do with God's will, not His weakness.

INTERPRETING THE SILENCE

Why do some of our prayers seemingly go unanswered? Just a few hours ago I sat with a young couple who asked that question not out of intellectual curiosity but from two broken hearts. As I write these words their baby son hovers between life and death with no great prospects of survival. And if he dies, they will bury their second child in the space of two years. They are filled with guilt, grief, deep disappointment – and a gnawing feeling that God simply doesn't like them very much.

They are not the first or the last to walk that lonely road. As we prayed and cried together, I simply encouraged them: 'Don't put the book down until the story is over.'

Many of the psalms express grief at disappointment and delay. Thankfully they are balanced by those that express joy and delight at answered prayer.

Our experience of prayers that are not answered straightaway – or are answered in a completely different way to what we expected – drives us back to what the Bible teaches. Prayer is about tuning our lives to God's purposes and presenting our needs and requests before a Father who knows best. For example, Paul, the Christian leader, carried the burden of personal pain and received an answer to his prayers that was not the one he wanted. But instead of it leaving him bitter and feeling rejected he found peace and acceptance. Take a look at 2 Corinthians 12:7–10 for Paul's personal account of how something that made him feel weak became a source of strength.

> 'Don't put the book down until the story is over'

Prayer is not a slot machine where we drop in a coin, pull a lever and get the answer we want. But it is a place where, like Hannah and Paul, we can bring our needs to a Father who cares. At such times when heaven seems silent we are cast back on some of the great truths from Scripture that fill the gaps and offer us hope. Look up these great verses from God's Word: Romans 8:28; Psalms 27; 34; Isaiah 43:1–4; Philippians 4:11–13.

If we see prayer as a means to getting what we want, we have misunderstood its purpose. It is about aligning our wills with God's will and has more to with discovering what He wants than getting what we want. There are times when what I ask for in prayer is just plain wrong or selfish ('O God let me win the lottery', for example). Or it may be that God is delaying His answer because there is a greater purpose still being worked out.

COMPLETING THE QUESTION

The question that heads this chapter is incomplete. Instead of asking 'Why are some prayers not answered?' I think it wise to add the words 'in the way we expect'.

I don't believe heaven is as silent as we think

I believe God does hear and answer our prayers. I don't believe heaven is as silent as we think. Think of Paul and his personal battle that we have briefly mentioned. He asked God to remove this problem (or thorn) from his life. His faith level was consistently high, he was a Christian leader with a proven track record and he had prayed for others many times – and seen God answer with miracles. In this instance, he didn't get a *no reply* from heaven – but he received an answer he didn't expect. He prayed for deliverance but was visited with grace instead.

God does hear His children when they pray – and calls

them to trust Him more when the answer they receive is not the one they expect. He has a greater plan that is being worked out and the good news is that the mysteries will one day become clear. The foggy mirror that we stare at will not always stay that way (see 1 Corinthians 13:12).

In the meantime we are called to walk by faith and to trust God even when we cannot understand Him. Faith and perplexity often walk together. Habakkuk, who lived around 600 years before Jesus, has a whole book in the Bible based on his personal struggle to understand God's big plan. He asks some tough and honest questions, finds a few answers and ends up in a place where he draws a line in the sand. *'Even when I can't work out what God is doing'*, he says, *'I will trust Him.'*

Reflect on his amazing declaration:

Though the fig-tree does not bud
and there are no grapes on the vines,
though the olive crop fails
and the fields produce no food,
though there are no sheep in the pen
and no cattle in the stalls,
yet I will rejoice in the LORD,
I will be joyful in God my Saviour.

The Sovereign LORD is my strength;
he makes my feet like the feet of a deer,
he enables me to go on the heights.
(Hab. 3:17–19)

The story of the mother that began this chapter highlights the dilemma we face when our prayers appear to go unanswered. The woman was called Monica and her wayward son a man called Augustine. Her fervent prayers were based on the belief that if he stayed close to her in Carthage she could influence him to become a follower of Christ. Her all-night vigil in the small chapel was her earnest attempt through prayer to reverse his plans to go and live in the city of Rome. His life was a big enough mess already and she feared that the bright lights of Rome would push him further from God's mercy.

We can only imagine Monica's grief when she left the chapel in the early morning to find Augustine had already sailed for Rome.

But in the greater purpose of God, it was in Rome he heard the great Christian leader Ambrose preaching and was deeply moved. It was in Rome, sitting in a garden, that he heard a child's voice shout, 'Take and read.' He picked up a copy of the New Testament that was lying there and read words that caused him to cry out to God for mercy.

Augustine (AD 354–430) is referred to as Augustine of Hippo – the city in North Africa where he served as Bishop. He became an influential thinker, writer, pastor and teacher and is widely regarded as one of the greats in the history of the Church. Among his books is *Confessions*, his account of his own spiritual journey, which has become a classic of world literature and an original work of philosophy.

Monica's prayers were answered – five years after that ship sailed, and in the city that she thought would lead Augustine away from Christ.

She discovered – as many do – that the Lord's ways are greater than ours and His purposes much, much wiser.

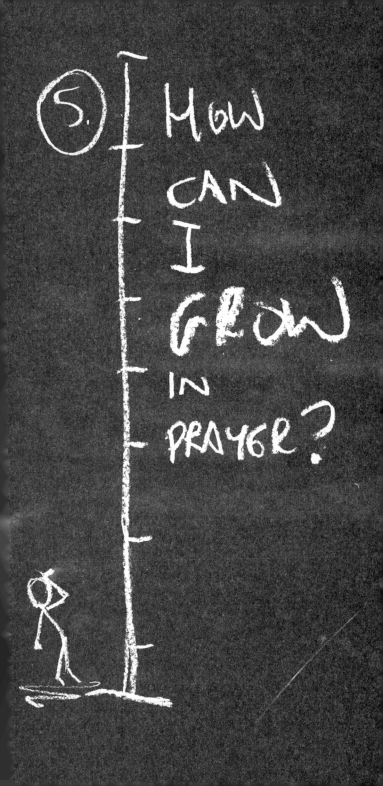

5. HOW CAN I GROW IN PRAYER?

You don't have to be around the Christian family very long before you discover that there are different ways of 'doing prayer'. Language, styles and patterns abound. In some countries the words 'let us pray' unleash a mighty torrent of noise as an entire congregation will pray out loud, together – and at length. For other Christians the only prayers they use are ones that someone else has written and the words are read from a book or sheet. Others believe it is better to pray off the cuff, yet from the heart, as they talk to God as clearly and honestly as they would to a friend at work. Some have a prayer language all of their own – either one given them by God or one inherited from people they admire.

Probably the most valuable lesson we learn from all this variety is that there is no one method that constitutes 'proper' prayer. If prayer at its simplest is conversation with God, then it seems HE is both multi-lingual and multi-cultural. What counts most is attitude, as the writer and poet Gerard Kelly expresses it:

> ... there are different ways of 'doing prayer'

Some pray like a BMW,
7 coats of shine and shimmer masking the hardness of steel
with an anti-emotion warranty to guard against the least sign of trust.
Some pray like a Porsche.
0 to victory in 6.7 seconds

banking on the promises of pray as you earn prosperity.
Jesus recommended praying in the garage, with the door shut,
engine and radio off,
praying when no-one is looking,
forgetting the traffic of the day,
meeting God in the quiet lay-by far from the pray and display.[1]

HOW DO YOU DO THAT?

The way Jesus prayed made an impression. His closest followers worked out the link between the time He spent praying (sometimes late at night after a long day or early morning before they were up and about) and the remarkable things that He did. Jesus specifically taught His disciples that prayer was a source of power. Take a look at Mark 9:28–29 where the disciples were puzzled and confused that they had been unable to drive out a demon. Jesus managed to do it and His followers asked Him privately why this was. He told them, 'This kind can come out only by prayer.'

So it is little wonder that one of Jesus' close circle made a special request, 'Lord, teach us to pray.' It is instructive to see how Jesus set about answering this cry from the heart (Luke 11:1–13).

Jesus starts with a reminder, moves on to tell a story, and ends with a promise – all of which make up a comprehensive lesson on how to grow in prayer.

A reminder
The first part of Jesus' reply is almost a repeat of the famous Lord's Prayer that He taught as part of the Sermon on the Mount. (See Chapter 3 – 'Is there a right way to

pray?' – where we looked at this famous prayer.) I use the word 'almost' because if we compare the version in Matthew with the one in Luke we notice that they are not identical. It is like the competition you find in a magazine where two photos or cartoons are placed side by side and readers are invited to spot the difference. Bible experts have done just that and drawn different conclusions as to why bits of the prayer are missing in Luke's version.

One explanation is that Jesus was reminding His enquiring friend about a prayer He had already taught. This unnamed disciple perhaps needed a reminder of the prayer, and its pattern for all our prayers, that Jesus had taught some time before.

Like children we are constantly dazzled by novelty – and things that are new do hold a special attraction. But we need to master the basics, and Jesus' initial response to the request for help is to remind His friend – and all disciples – of what he already knew. If we are serious about growing in our prayer lives then it seems that getting back to first principles is a good place to start.

... getting back to first principles is a good place to start

A story

According to Luke, Jesus followed up this reminder with a story to illustrate a point. This parable is known as *The Friend at Midnight* and is best understood by those who are familiar with the habit of hospitality that runs through many cultures. In the world of Jesus' day, offering food, drink and shelter was accepted behaviour – even if the guests were not immediate family. That idea runs through the parable and lends us understanding.

The story has a semi-comical feel. A man gets an unexpected late-night visit from a friend who is on a journey. But his larder is empty and he has nothing to offer his guest in the way of food. So, in the middle of the night, he calls on a neighbour who is also a friend and asks a favour – could he borrow some bread?

Picture the scene as Jesus paints it. A whole family living in a single room, bedded down and asleep. The natural response would be to shout out, 'Go away and stop making a racket! We're trying to sleep.' But according to Jesus, the man wearily stumbles around in the dark, lights a lamp and finds the bread his friend has asked for.

Why? That is the question this story raises. Why on earth should friendship stretch so far that this man is willing to put himself out for a demanding friend? Listen to Jesus make a telling point:

> 'I tell you, though he will not get up and give him the
> bread because he is his friend, yet because of the man's
> boldness he will get up and give him as much as he needs.'
> (Luke 11:8)

Notice that word 'boldness', because it is the key word in the story; it sums up an attitude that is shameless and full of cheek. The Greek word is *anaideia* and it denotes recklessness. The adjective related to this word describes a person who shows no restraint or deference. Tim Chester takes a different tack by saying the word doesn't apply to the man knocking, but to the man asleep in bed:

> He answers because he does not want to bring shame
> on himself by refusing the request and tarnishing the

village's reputation for hospitality. He is the centre of the parable and the one whose attitude casts light on the attitude of God … [Jesus] is not saying that God is like a reluctant neighbour who has to be nagged before he will do anything for us. Rather, he is saying, if a reluctant human being will give you what you want out of concern for his reputation, *how much more* will your loving Heavenly Father? If a man will answer your cry even though he is asleep with his family, *how much more* will he who never sleeps? God is ready to hear us. Our Father is willing to hear our prayers.[2]

The implications of Jesus' words jar. Is this how we are to approach God in prayer, in some rude, brash fashion? As a master communicator, Jesus is making a startling point. He is tackling two of the biggest barriers we face in prayer and urging us to knock them aside. These two barriers block us from growing in prayer:

> ... God invites our prayers

- We are blocked by the feeling that God is too big and busy to worry about our trivial concerns.
- We are hindered by thinking, 'If everything is already planned – what's the point of praying?'

When such thoughts trouble us we are reminded of the friend who possessed such a nerve that he could go and knock on his neighbour's door in the middle of the night. The heart of the story is this: God invites our prayers.

A promise
This stunning lesson on prayer draws to a conclusion with a series of promises which – if they did not come

from the lips of Jesus – we would consider blasphemous. God, our Father, invites us to bring our needs to Him and promises to answer according to His will. We can trust Him because He cares for us. Look at how *The Message* paraphrase expresses these promises:

> We can trust Him because He cares for us

'Ask and you'll get;
Seek and you'll find;
Knock and the door will open.'

'Don't bargain with God. Be direct. Ask for what you need. This is not a cat-and-mouse, hide-and-seek game we're in. If your little boy asks for a serving of fish, do you scare him with a live snake on his plate? If your little girl asks for an egg do you trick her with a spider? As bad as you are, you wouldn't think of such a thing – you're at least decent to your own children. And don't you think the Father who conceived you in love will give the Holy Spirit when you ask him?'
(Luke 11:9–13)

GROWING IN PRAYER

With the words of Jesus ringing in our ears we are encouraged to grow in prayer. But how do we set about moving on from where we are?

At the time of writing this, my wife and I are getting ready to move abroad. We are going to work with a church in Geneva that is based a few hundred metres from the border on the French side. Because it is an international church, English is the common language, but we will be living in a French community and will need to develop our language skills.

Now we know a little French (like most Christians would say they know a bit about prayer), but we have not studied it since we were at school. On our holidays we have got by with some tourist-speak and have developed what we call 'team French' – between the two of us we have enough vocabulary to hold a basic conversation!

So we are now facing the fact that we need to grow and make a conscious effort to improve our linguistic abilities. I am learning about three things that make a difference:

1. Motivation

Dieting, learning a language – or growing in my prayer life – all begin with a desire to change. I need to want to reach a certain goal and be willing to focus my energies on achieving it. It is summed up in the passage we have just considered when an unnamed disciple said to Jesus, 'Lord, teach us to pray.'

Beginning with that honest request is the first step on the road to developing a richer prayer life.

2. Help

Desire without direction ends in frustration. The intention of my wife and I to become more fluent in French has set us off in several directions.

Self-help has been invaluable as we have started to read and listen to different courses.

Trained help is on hand as we enrol for language classes in France and commit ourselves to weekly attendance.

Supportive help comes from friends who have trod the same path and offer encouragement, advice and those wonderful words of reassurance: 'You can do it.'

Such help can move us forward in our prayer life. Reading books, listening to messages and asking friends about their experiences in prayer are all avenues of practical help. A good question to ask a Christian friend is, 'What has been the biggest help in your prayer life?' If you are part of a house group ask that question, notice the variety of answers and use the ones most suited to you.

3. Practice

I remember when I was at school, struggling with Latin – a subject that never made any sense to me. I took great comfort in the rhyme: 'Latin is a language as dead as dead can be, It killed the ancient Romans – and now it's killing me!'

But French is a living language, thankfully, and as every language teacher knows, the best way to grow in confidence is to get out and use it. Your vocabulary, accent and understanding all improve when you get out into the big wide world and use what you have been learning.

Prayer is a special gift for all God's children

We grow in prayer when we practise it. That may involve rescheduling your daily timetable to create space to pray, or finding a couple of friends who will commit to meet with you regularly to pray, or deciding to attend a prayer meeting. The important thing is that our good intentions are translated into action.

Motivation, help and practice are three vital ingredients that help us grow in knowledge and skill for many things in life – from bee keeping to French polishing. And they also apply to developing our prayer life. I am not suggesting for a minute that prayer is 'just a hobby', but I am trying to remove some of the mystique that sometimes surrounds it.

Prayer is a special gift for all God's children – not just a favoured few. Billy Graham reminded us that not all discover this truth when he said, 'Heaven is full of answers to prayers for which no one ever bothered to ask.'

So if you want to grow in prayer, begin by asking, 'Lord, teach me to pray.'

NOTES
1. Gerard Kelly, *The Games People Pray*
2. Tim Chester *The Message of Prayer, The Bible Speaks Today – Bible Themes Series* (Leicester: IVP, 2003) p.46. Used with permission.

6.

WHAT DOES A PRAYING CHURCH LOOK LIKE?

6. WHAT DOES A PRAYING CHURCH LOOK LIKE?

Browsing through an antique shop recently I came across a large collection of photographs and postcards that someone had taken the time and trouble to index according to topics and places. It was fascinating to look at pictures taken decades earlier, note the change in fashions and speculate concerning the circumstances surrounding a particular photo.

When we come to examine this particular FAQ – what does a praying church look like? – it's a case of back to the future. There are many contemporary examples of what we could broadly call prayer movements: prayer mountains in Korea, local churches that have undertaken 24/7 prayer initiatives and marches such as the world-famous March for Jesus.

We can learn much about prayer by looking at a couple of 'old photographs' in the New Testament that give us a snapshot of how the first Christians regarded the vital subject of prayer. First we will take a look at the energetic, visionary church in Antioch and, second, at some advice given to a young Christian pastor concerning the importance of prayer in a local church.

A VISIONARY CHURCH

Antioch was the third largest city in the Roman Empire, ranked after Rome and Alexandria. It boasted a population of 500,000 people from many parts of the known world – it was a truly cosmopolitan city. It stood near the mouth of the Orontes River, fifteen miles from the Mediterranean Sea, and was famous for gambling and an extravagant style of living. One writer paints a vivid picture:

> [Antioch] was famous for her chariot racing and a kind of deliberate pursuit of pleasure which went on literally night and day. To put it in modern terms, we might describe her as a city of sport run mad, of betting, gambling and nightclubs.[1]

The gospel of Jesus came to this predominantly non-Jewish city and made a great impact. The book of Acts describes the origins and rapid growth of the church at Antioch (Acts 11:19–26). This was the place where the name 'Christian' was first coined and the congregation quickly grew to become a thriving international church with far-sighted vision.

Recorded in Acts are details of a leadership prayer meeting that paved the way to a major shift in the understanding and activities of the Early Christian Church. Under the leadership of Barnabas, the team at Antioch had grown and the picture painted is of a multi-gifted, multi-national leadership (see Acts 13:1–3).

As the leaders gave time to worship and prayer they received a message through the Holy Spirit. It was a specific instruction for two of the team to be set aside for a special task and, following further prayer, they sent Barnabas and Saul off to share the Christian message wherever the Lord directed. The brief incident begs many questions that we are unable to answer – but several things are clear. Here was a group of leaders who gave serious time and effort to prayer, listened hard to God and followed the directions they received.

Antioch is sometimes referred to as 'the first missional church' or 'the first missionary congregation'. The Christians there were the launch pad for a conscious expansion effort for the message about Jesus and through their obedient faith other churches came into being through the missionary endeavours of Barnabas and Saul – the latter becoming better know as Paul.

A BUSY PASTOR

A second 'photo' from the pages of the New Testament is a segment from a letter written to a young Christian leader. The leader's name was Timothy and the letter came from his mentor and spiritual father, Paul.

Timothy was leading the church at Ephesus at this time and he faced quite a few challenges. The letter (1 Timothy) is one of the so-called 'pastoral epistles' that set out some of the priorities of pastoring Christ's Church. It seems there were some (possibly leaders) in the church who were caught up in unnecessary conflicts and arguments over obscure issues. Paul wasted no time in telling his colleague how to deal with such people. (See 1 Timothy 1:3–7. For a helpful explanation of the nature of the issue Timothy faced see Tim Chester, *The Message of Prayer.*[2])

Local church life hasn't changed that much in two thousand years. There have been and always will be controversial issues that threaten to divide the people of God. Timothy faced some people in his church who were bent on majoring over minors, it would appear that the line they took was based on some 'new discovery' that Paul viewed as speculative, unnecessary, introspective and divisive. We may not know all the details but we can get the general drift. But what is most helpful is to see how Timothy is told to deal with the matter. Paul's letter is packed with wise advice about how to steer a church through such choppy waters, including the importance of having good leaders in place.

But right at the heart of this advice – one might suggest at the top of the list – comes a call to prayer.

'I urge, then, first of all, that requests, prayers, intercession and thanksgiving be made for everyone – for kings and all those in authority, that we might live peaceful and quiet lives in all godliness and holiness … I want men everywhere to lift up holy hands in prayer, without anger or disputing.' (1 Tim. 2:1–2,8)

Paul urges his young protégé to ensure that prayer is put into a more central place in the life of the church at Ephesus. They were big on talk and short on prayer, and Paul seeks to redress the balance. But notice that it is a call to prayer that is broad – four different words are used to describe a single activity. Some have speculated at length about the difference and relationship between these prayer activities. But it appears Paul is not giving a seminar on types of prayer as much as saying, 'However you do it – just do it!' It is instructive that the prayer called for is outward looking – too many Christians pray through very selfish shopping lists. Paul is urging them to look at the world around and even pray for the pagan Roman emperor. He also sees prayer – serious prayer – as an antidote to angry Christian in-fighting.

There is a deep lesson here that we would do well to learn. The church at Ephesus had lost the plot and their time was being consumed by trivial pursuits. Timothy's task as a leader was to restore a sense of focus – and prayer was an important element in this process.

LEARNING FROM THE FAMILY HISTORY

Antioch saw its whole ministry change shape through prayer – and Timothy was urged to tackle some serious problems at Ephesus by restoring prayer to a more central place. So what can we learn from our roots about the profile of a praying church?

1. A praying church gives a central place to prayer

At Antioch the leadership gave themselves to worship with fasting and prayer, while at Ephesus it would seem they had lost focus because prayer had slipped from that central place. How we express the central importance of prayer will vary according to our tradition, culture and practice of prayer. But a praying church prays – not simply talks about it or acknowledges it in a statement of faith.

2. A praying church sees prayer as a whole communication process

Prayer is not simply us talking to God – it involves active listening too, working on our simple definition: prayer is conversation with God. But the strongest relationships come where there is listening as well as talking. The Antioch church received a startling message – it may well have been one that took them a bit by surprise. It was costly for them to part with two of their most gifted leaders with no sense of how long they'd be gone, who would check up

> Prayer ... involves active listening too

on them and a host of other practical things. In contrast, the congregation at Ephesus were suffering from some leaders who were 'off message' because they were tuning in to the wrong voices.

69

3. A praying church sees prayer as the place where vision is born

A praying church doesn't have months of discussion, take a decision and then as an afterthought offer a quick prayer for blessing. Vision comes through prayer and is fed and watered by prayer. The Antioch church offers a stunning example of what can happen when a church listens to God and steps out in faith and obedience. Meanwhile Timothy's job at Ephesus was to steer the church away from unhelpful speculation and argument back into the heart of God's plan for them as they tried to live for Christ in a strongly pagan environment.

4. A praying church gives prayer an outward focus

A survey of British Christians revealed that the majority of their prayers were for personal needs or for those in their immediate circle. There is nothing wrong with such prayers – the Bible teaches us to bring our needs to God in prayer. But if all our praying is about ourselves there is something missing. Look at Paul's instruction to Timothy: prayer is to be comprehensive and based on God's love for people, and His desire to see them come to saving faith in Jesus Christ. Our prayers need to have a mission shape too.

5. A praying church is alert to the constant need not to let prayer slip

Like a yachtsman at the helm, we need to be constantly checking our course and correcting it where necessary. There are always lots of good ideas and worthy causes. If we are not careful we can run the risk of trying to do too many things and ending up doing them badly. 'Do less but do it better' is wise advice. Constantly ensuring that prayer is central will save a church from chaotic activity that leads nowhere.

D.L. Moody wrote: 'Every great movement of God can be traced to a kneeling figure' and the famous Victorian preacher Charles Spurgeon told his London congregation, 'May God help me if you cease to pray for me! Let me know the day, and I must cease to preach.' Both men witnessed thousands coming to personal faith in Christ through their preaching.

But as their comments suggest, they knew that powerful preaching was the result of persistent praying.

NOTES
1. William Barclay, *The Daily Study Bible, The Acts of the Apostles* (Edinburgh: St Andrews Press, 1955) p.94.
2. Tim Chester, *The Message of Prayer, The Bible Speaks Today – Bible Themes Series* (Leicester: IVP, 2003) pp.206ff.

7. DOES PRAYER CHANGE THINGS?

In the film *The Truman Show*, Jim Carrey plays the part of Truman Burbank – a man whose life is one giant illusion. What he thinks is normal life is in fact a TV show created inside a false world within a giant dome. Day, night, the weather and temperature are all controlled artificially. Truman is the only one who doesn't know this – everyone in his life is an actor. Five thousand cameras record his life twenty-four hours a day, seven days a week. Truman Burbank is a prisoner of illusion.

His suspicions are aroused by a series of incidents that prompt him to discover the truth. And when he finds his life is not real he opts to escape, trading unreality for uncertainty. He chooses to escape and find a real life rather than a make-believe one.

Some view people of faith as being like Truman Burbank – well-meaning souls trapped in a religious world that is a giant illusion. Prayer, they would claim, is but a symptom of such poor souls' sickness.

Does prayer change things? Are we are simply deluding ourselves when we pray? Are we guilty of self-deception? Does prayer work? We move to our final 'frequently asked question' about prayer.

'CO-INCIDENCE' AND 'GOD-INCIDENCE'

Too many people have experienced remarkable answers to prayer for their views to be dismissed. These answers are sometimes described as 'God-incidences' because to put them down to 'co-incidence' would be to ignore the significant part played through prayer. And then there are the beneficial effects of prayer on those who exercise faith. As Pablo Martinez has written:

> As an observer of human nature and as a Christian professional in psychotherapy, I can testify to the psychotherapeutic effects of prayer. No secular psychologist, who considers him or herself to be impartial and sensible, can deny the unparalleled therapeutic value of faith in general and of prayer in particular.[1]

To dismiss prayer as make-believe supporting a fantasy is to fly in the face of the evidence. Far from producing escapists, prayer instils courage, strength and perseverance causing people to rise above themselves and achieve remarkable things. And as for the answers to prayer – there are just too many for them to be described as mere coincidence. 'God-incidence' would appear to be a more accurate description.

ANOTHER PRAYER LESSON FROM JESUS

To help us answer the question, 'Does prayer change things?', we are going to look at another prayer lesson Jesus taught His followers. This is based on the account given in Mark 11:12–25.

At first reading the incident is difficult to understand. It is made up of three separate but linked incidents that occur in the space of twenty-four hours.

Jesus is in the final week before His betrayal and execution. In Mark's account this all takes place on the Monday and Tuesday before Good Friday.

Three separate events occur:

• The cursing of a fig tree

- The cleaning up of the Temple
- The practical lesson about prayer

The cursing of a fig tree

Jesus and His close team had stayed overnight in Bethany and, in the morning, walked the relatively short journey to the bustling city of Jerusalem. Jesus was hungry and examined a fig tree in leaf for some fruit – only to find there was nothing to eat. So, in the hearing of His disciples, He said to the tree 'May no-one ever eat fruit from you again' (Mark 11:14). Mark swiftly shifts the scene to the city of Jerusalem and, in particular, the Temple.

But in the space of a few verses he returns to this curious incident with the fig tree.

The next morning – twenty-four hours on from Jesus' cursing of the bare tree – Peter makes a startling observation. The tree has withered from its roots. With astonishment, he draws Jesus' attention to this amazing sight. Jesus makes no specific comment on the fate of the tree but uses it to illustrate the importance of faith in God and the enormous power that is found through prayer.

But surely it was unreasonable for Jesus to look for fruit when, according to Mark, it was not even the season for figs? All is not as it appears. Jesus knew that this particular tree would be all leaves and no fruit because the signs were already there. Some have suggested that leaves had appeared on the tree without any sign of the precursors to the true figs (the precursors are in Palestinian Arabic called *taqsh*). These precursors are a sign that there will be no figs. Since Jesus found 'nothing but leaves' – leaves without any *taqsh* – He knew that it was an absolutely hopeless, fruitless fig tree, and said as much. This explanation is more fully discussed by W.M.

Christie in *The Barren Fig Tree*.[2]

He didn't curse it in a fit of pique but as what we call an 'enacted parable'. And to understand that we need to look at the details of His visit to the Temple of which the Jewish nation was so proud.

The cleaning up of the Temple

The significance of the incident becomes clearer when we consider Jesus' actions at the Temple. The fig tree, full of leaves but empty of fruit, was a picture of the spiritual state of Israel. Mark records that Jesus entered the Temple courts and immediately created a disturbance by driving out the tradesmen, overturning the money-changers' tables and the benches of those selling birds for sacrifice. He also stopped people carrying goods through the Temple area as it had become a short cut into the city.

This must have been a vivid scene and one that we somehow struggle to equate with the idea of Jesus as the man of love and peace. The reason for His indignant actions is explained by two verses from the Old Testament Scriptures that the Jewish worshippers claimed to know so well.

God's intention for the Temple was this: 'My house will be called a house of prayer for all nations' (Isa. 56:7) but instead 'you have made it a den of robbers' (Jer. 7:11). By placing these two quotes together – the first from Isaiah and the second from Jeremiah – Jesus was delivering a verdict on the spiritual state of the nation God had chosen to bring blessing to the world.

What was taking place at the Temple was a symptom of the spiritual sickness of Israel. The Temple courts had been turned into a marketplace and some people were more interested in making money than worshipping God. There were stalls everywhere offering animals and birds for sacrifice. The only money accepted in the Temple was the shekel, so foreign money – which had the hated figure of Caesar on it – was banned. To worship, you had to convert coinage and the money-changers enjoyed a healthy mark-up. According to Jesus, people were being robbed spiritually as well as financially. Their religion was about what they got out of it, rather than about offering themselves to God.

Jesus' violent outburst made its mark. Many were amazed at His words and actions – but the religious establishment realised that they could not let Him live any longer. Jesus needed to be disposed of – permanently.

The practical lesson about prayer

The link between the cursing of the fig tree and the cleaning up of the Temple is that Israel was like the fruitless tree. God's judgment would fall and this Temple – of which the Jewish nation was so proud – would also fall. God was doing a new thing and many had failed to perceive it. Jesus' action over the tree was a prophetic enactment of what would happen within a generation to the Temple. It was completely destroyed by the Romans in AD 70.

... faith and prayer go together

Peter's astonishment over the withered tree prompts Jesus to give another lesson on prayer. He makes two important points about faith and forgiveness.

1. Faith – Jesus tells Peter that faith and prayer go together. Most importantly, it is not any vague belief but faith in God that counts. That type of faith can move mountains. The rabbis of Jesus' day often referred to big problems as 'mountains', so in using this figure of

speech Jesus is saying *Even the biggest things you face can be moved through prayer.* Jesus underlines this with a promise: 'Therefore I tell you, whatever you ask for in prayer, believe that you have received it, and it will be yours' (Mark 11:24).

2. Forgiveness – Hot on the heels of this remarkable promise, Jesus adds a reminder about the need to forgive others. Unless we are prepared to forgive, we cannot be forgiven. Our attitudes towards others really do affect our prayers and Peter (who was the focus of this lesson, it seems) obviously understood this deeply. Years later, as a leader of the Church, he warns husbands that the way they treated their wives would affect their prayers being heard and answered: 'Husbands, in the same way be considerate as you live with your wives and treat them with respect as the weaker partner and as heirs with you of the gracious gift of life, so that nothing will hinder your prayers' (1 Pet. 3:7).

> Our attitudes towards others really do affect our prayers

Perhaps a reason more 'mountains' are not moved through our prayers is that an unforgiving heart hinders the flow of faith.

Mountain-moving prayer

There was a slogan popular among Christians years ago: 'Prayer changes things'. I have puzzled over the years as to whether it is actually true. I believe in the power of prayer and have seen many wonderful answers – but my personal experience and observation of others leads me to want to change the slogan slightly. I believe *God changes things* and I also believe *prayer is powerful.*

You may think I am being pedantic and fussing over nothing – but consider the prayer lesson I've outlined above. Jesus didn't say to Peter, *'have faith in prayer'* – but rather *'have faith in God'*. The distinction is important: God is the source and prayer is the connection.

This is where some people miss the plot by believing that by following a formula or style the answer to a prayer is bound to come. If it doesn't, then there must be a blockage of some kind, and often the person being prayed for is accused of unconfessed sin or a lack of faith. This heaps guilt on the head of someone who is already struggling under a heavy load, and makes him or her feel even further away from God and His transforming love.

The answer to any prayer lies in God's hands. That is why our praying must always be according to His will and purpose rather than our own. As someone once put it, 'We can only move mountains that God wants removed – not those that we want moved.'

There are four answers that God gives to a prayer:

- Yes
- No
- Wait
- Here is something better.

Maturity is the ability not only to understand the answer, but most of all to accept it. Such understanding should not blunt our prayers but serve to sharpen them to greater keenness.

Mountain-moving prayer is about growing closer to the Lord, involving Him in the details of our lives, seeking His wise intervention through our prayers and watching with wonder and worship as He works His will in and through us, for His glory.

An unknown Confederate soldier, who fought in the American Civil War in the 1860s, composed this prayer and left it as a written testimony to the power of God through the power of prayer. It reminds us that God does hear and answer prayer. But as a loving Father, He always gives us what we need rather than what we want.

I asked God for strength that I might achieve,
I was made weak that I might learn humbly to obey.
I asked for health that I might do greater things,
I was given infirmity that I might do better things.
I asked for riches that I might be happy,
I was given poverty that I might be wise.
I asked for power that I might have the praise of men,
I was given weakness that I might feel the need of God.
I asked for all things that I might enjoy life,
I was given life that I might enjoy all things.
I was given nothing I asked for,
but everything that I had hoped for.
Despite myself, my prayers were answered.
I am among all men most richly blessed.

Does prayer change things? No – God does. But prayer is the tool He puts into our hands.

NOTES

1. Pablo Martinez, *Prayer Life – How personality affects the way you pray* (Carlisle: Spring Harvest Publishing Division and Paternoster Lifestyle, 2002) p.77. Used with permission.

2. W.M. Christie, discussion entitled *The Barren Fig Tree*, quoted in Walter C. Kaiser Jr, Peter H. Davids, F.F. Bruce and Manfred T. Brauch, *Hard Sayings of the Bible* (Downers Grove, Illinois: IVP, 1996).

P.S.

P.S.

When I was about eight years old I had my first experience of being conned. An older boy showed me a magic bush on the route home from school and told me if I shared some of my pocket money with him and wished really hard, then whatever gifts I wanted would magically appear in the middle of the bush within twenty-four hours. I gladly gave him the money and set about sharing a long list of things I wanted. Believe me, an eight-year-old boy can think of a lot of things he wants.

Twenty-four hours later I could hardly wait for school to end as I rushed up the road and began to eagerly explore the heart of the bush. It was big, thick and prickly and I ended up dirty, sweaty and scratched. I also ended up a lot wiser.

At the tender age of eight I discovered there is no such thing as a magic bush.

I have met some who have had the same experience with prayer. They mistakenly think it is a magic bush – ask for whatever you want and you'll get it. They didn't, and so concluded that prayer doesn't work – and probably God doesn't exist.

But – as I hope this short book has uncovered – there is no 'magic bush' about prayer. God has given us this amazing gift as a way that we can get to know, understand and experience Him. Fundamentally, prayer is about our relationship with Jesus Christ.

Whilst writing this book, I asked some friends to share something they have learned about prayer in their own journey of faith. When I read their responses I knew they should be included at the end of the book. They remind us that prayer is about a relationship with God – a relationship through which we can learn and grow. And it is through this relationship that we can discover how He works and how we can partner Him in His plans.

Prayer is not just about getting what I want. It is about discovering what God wants.

I hope that reading what my friends have written will stimulate and inspire you to pray with faith and to see what God can do.

To set the ball rolling, I will share two things that I have learned/am learning about prayer.

1. PRAY WITH OTHERS

I have found that praying with other people really helps – especially when my faith and self-discipline are weak. I have been part of different prayer groups determined according to my work and where I have been living. One group I shared with for fifteen years, and learned much through the relationships we formed. Currently I pray with someone on a regular basis, and we walk and pray at the same time, figuring that spiritual and bodily exercise go well together!

2. WRITE DOWN WHAT YOU PRAY

I have found it helpful to write the names of some of the people I am praying for and what I am asking God to do in their lives. It is also good for me to write down specific answers to prayer. These reminders build my faith at times when I feel discouraged. They also provide written monuments to God's faithfulness.

I trust you will find what follows helpful – and, most of all, that it will encourage you to pray and not give up.

ROB FROST
Director, Share Jesus International

My view of intercession has changed over the years. I used to think of it as a kind of shopping list of need, for me, my loved ones and the world. But now I see it less as words and more as expressing my deepest feelings to Jesus.

I'm with Paul when he wrote, 'We do not know what we ought to pray for, but the Spirit himself intercedes for us with groans that words cannot express. And he who searches our hearts knows the mind of the Spirit, because the Spirit intercedes for the saints in accordance with God's will' (Rom. 8:26–27).

When I come to the 'holy place' where Jesus is seated at the right hand of the Father, then, I don't believe He wants me to gabble a list of things I want Him to do. He knows the list before I arrive, anyway. No, He wants to read my heart. He wants to see if I care, to know I feel the burden and to recognise that I am emotionally engaged with what I'm asking Him to do.

When I pray for others now I'm less concerned about getting the words in the right order, and much more interested in 'feeling' the needs I'm expressing.

RUSSELL ROOK
Director, ALOVE, The Salvation Army for a new generation

'Prayer is not a calling upon the God who isn't involved. Prayer is keeping up with the God who is already involved.'

As my teacher, Dr Murray Rae, moved on to theological pastures new, I remember choosing to rest a moment with what I had just heard. Even now, five years on, I come back to the quote over and over again. And while I have many unoriginal questions concerning our ability to change God's mind, how many times we must ask for something before we get it and whether God's answers display favouritism or arbitrary choice, I do know that prayer has a unique effect upon my discipleship and, with the help of the wider tradition of the Church, I have made the life-changing discovery that prayer is about far more than my self-baptised, consumerist wishlist.

R.T. KENDALL
Writer, preacher and former Senior Minister of Westminster Chapel, London

What I have discovered about prayer:
1. Time with God is never wasted.
2. I have learned more of God's ways by spending a lot of time in His presence.
3. My anointing increases when I pray more, it diminishes when I pray less.
4. I am easier to live with when I have had adequate time alone with the Lord.
5. Insights into Scripture increase when I pray more.
6. Prayer and Bible reading are as equally needed as sunshine and rain.
7. The more I pray, the more I get done.
8. Taking time to thank God for things is as important as petitions.
9. If you don't know how to spend more time in prayer, get a prayer list and keep adding to it.
10. Intercession for others via a prayer list does as much good for my soul, or more, as praying for myself.

PETER MAIDEN
International Director, OM International

Conversation with my Lord throughout the day is a very real and special experience for me. But I believe I need more than that. Jesus gave concentrated periods of time to be with His Father. I know I need and want that. But to discipline myself to get these times and to truly use them, I find a constant struggle. From experiencing much failure I have learned the following. First, I need to get these times firmly into my diary and give them priority. Second, I need to prepare these times. I need the right place and to plan the use of my time, otherwise I'll spend more time dreaming of England retaining the Ashes. Thirdly, I need variety in these times. Recent important additions, for me, for example, have been the importance of periods of silence and listening rather than speaking, and the use of liturgy. I'm still failing, still trying, because I believe such times are of vital importance.

DEREK TIDBALL
College Principal, London School of Theology

The most important thing I have discovered about prayer is that we need to demystify it. It is simply a conversation between friends and should be as rich and varied, as committed and supportive, as robust and honest as conversations between friends are.

Yet, if it is a conversation between friends, it is not a conversation between equals. God is by far the senior partner in the friendship. His power is awesome; His being is holy; His will is supreme; and His grace is sufficient. If it were not so, it would be pointless talking with Him. The only true foundation of our conversation – as the great intercessors like Abraham, David, Daniel and Nehemiah show – is His character and His covenant love. Our praying should be much more of Him and less of us than it often is.

DOTHA BLACKWOOD
Lecturer in Theology and Biblical Studies and Director of Practical Training, Moorlands College

Hmm! Where do I begin …? Having grown up in a very large Pentecostal Church (in Jamaica) I learnt very early that in order to be effective (or rather, to be any sort of 'proper' Christian) one had to be a person of prayer. Prayer meetings were a weekly event; ALL NIGHT prayer meetings were also a regular monthly feature! Then there was the annual month of prayer and fasting which, as a leader, one was expected to attend. One was also encouraged to 'get up early in the mornings' and 'start the day right' – with an hour (at least) of prayer.

For years I did the 'attending' bit, and the 'trying to pray like the others' bit and 'to encourage others to do so' bit too, until one day (several years ago now) I just said out loud (as I walked down the streets of Kingston), 'God, I really can't be bothered with all this. It's just not working!' Imagine my surprise when, very clearly, I heard God say, 'GOOD! Now we can talk!' Me being me, I replied, 'What, you mean just – talk?'

To cut a long journey/story short, since then I have discovered that prayer is really simply that – TALKING TO GOD, and allowing God to respond in the way that God knows is best. I learnt from, and have come to appreciate the honesty of, the psalmists who didn't always feel like things were going their way and were HONEST about it, while still acknowledging God as Sovereign Lord.

Jeremiah is also a favourite of mine. He had some serious conversations with God and, at times, seemed to 'batter God on the chest' with his (Jeremiah's) dissatisfaction with the way things were. What I noticed was that God didn't seem to mind that. Jeremiah didn't always like the reply (when there was one!) but he was honest. That's probably the most valuable lesson about prayer I've learnt over the years: I can be (in the words of J.A.T. Robinson) HONEST TO GOD! He isn't some ogre in the sky waiting to see if, when or what I pray before deciding if He should 'bash me over the head'. He is a gracious, loving Father who says 'Come to Me.'

I have also learnt, finally, that prayer is also a discipline, and that it helps to have routines, but that one should not feel, or be, condemned when life, death and other eventualities interrupt the routine. Oh, and by the way – getting up early to pray is not such a bad thing!!!

STEVE BRADY
Principal, Moorlands College

I have learned that 'No' is an answer to prayer. My wife Brenda was just thirty when we discovered that she had a medical condition for which there is no cure: multiple sclerosis. Over the years, it is true to say that thousands of Christians have prayed for her healing, and a number directly with and over her. Twenty-seven years on, she still has MS, with all its progressively destructive power.

Some fellow Christians find this hard: why hasn't God healed her? Is it our lack of faith? Some unconfessed sin? A curse on our family tree? Pastorally speaking, most of those well-intentioned probes are a road to spiritual despair. Isn't it possible that the Lord has some other purpose in mind through this process? I think so.

Over the years, verses from the Bible have at times leapt out and sustained us: 'When you pass through the waters, I will be with you …' (Isa. 43:2); 'This sickness will not end in death. No, it is for God's glory …' (John 11:4); 'You do not realise now what I am doing, but later you will understand' (John 13:7). Perhaps, however, no verses are more clear than those that speak of Paul's desire to be free from whatever was his 'thorn in the flesh'. Even though he had pleaded with the Lord for its removal on more than one occasion, the reply was startling:

'My grace is sufficient for you, for my power is made perfect in weakness' (see 2 Cor. 12:7–10).

As an earthly father, without claiming infallibility – my kids think I did, regularly! – there were times when they could not fathom my 'No' to their insistent 'must have now'. I don't know the reasons why God answers prayer by saying 'No' sometimes. But I have learned that Father really does know best, and grants 'strength for today and bright hope for tomorrow' in Christ. One day, I'll be glad for prayers answered by His 'No'.

CELIA BOWRING
Prayer Co-ordinator, Care

Surroundings are significant for me. I love to take a solitary walk or find a quiet room with plenty of time to read the Bible and then share with God whatever's on my mind and heart. Inevitably, this is not always a reality, so most days I 'pray in bursts' as opportunities arise and particular needs occur to me.

Everyone's different, but I love to praise God when worshipping in a lively congregation, enjoying personal communion with Him at the same time. This interface of public and private is important, whether in a prayer meeting or a church service, to be 'me' as well as 'we' in God's presence.

Lastly, although I never manage a spiritual journal for more than a week, I find writing prayers enormously satisfying and enjoy reading those composed by others. As I grow older I find church liturgy increasingly beautiful and profound.

ROB PARSONS
Executive Director, Care for the Family

It was Alec Motyer, the famous Scottish preacher, who said, 'If God was committed to answer all my prayers with a "Yes", then I would never have the courage to pray for anything ever again.' I think he's right. If God had answered all my prayers that way, I would have married the girl with bright ginger hair who I fell in love with when I was eleven. But as I've got older I have had deeper cause to be grateful that the Almighty is not bound to grant every petition.

I find that one of the strange things about age is that I revisit songs I used to sing in Sunday school, but with fresh understanding. Here's part of one which Miss Williams, my Sunday school teacher, taught me:

God holds the key to all unknown and I am glad.
If other hands should hold the key,
Or if He trusted it to me,
I might be sad.

Lord, in your mercy, keep that key in Your hand.

ROSEMARY CONLEY
Diet and Fitness Expert

I really value my early morning prayer time and always feel that it sets me up for the day. I wish I was as disciplined with my exercise! It was twenty years ago that I invited Jesus into my life and prayer soon became part of my daily routine. I find having a prayer list helpful and encouraging, particularly when I find old ones in the back of a drawer and realise how many of those prayers have been answered. I also find that telling people I have prayed for them, or that they are on my daily prayer list, really encourages them.

My father always prayed in the early morning and regularly met with a homegroup from his church on Tuesday evenings. My mother had gone to be with the Lord some two years previously and father was living alone. One morning during his prayer time, he felt God tell him that he should marry Mabel, a member of the homegroup. Father was sixty-nine and Mabel, having nursed and cared for her mother and father until they had died some years previously, was unmarried and fifty-one.

Father, excited by the Lord's revelation, immediately walked down to Mabel's house a few doors away and told her the news! Mabel, who had not had a boyfriend even when younger, needless to say was somewhat shocked. Apparently father said he would go down to the town for his shopping and would come back shortly for an answer!

Four months later Mabel and father were married and lived a totally devoted life together until he died at the grand age of eighty-eight. Mabel nursed him lovingly through several heart-breaking years as his gradual-onset Alzheimer's took over his life until he died.

Perhaps father's ability to hear from God so clearly, his obedience and Mabel's trust in God, are lessons for us all.

DAVID COFFEY
President, Baptist World Alliance

Turning the duty of prayer into a delight depends on being disciplined about prayer. I use trigger points to stimulate prayer. The first cup of tea of the day is a trigger point for my wife and me to pray for family and friends. Walking the family dog a few years ago, I designated a prayer post in a field and a thinking bridge over a stream, as places where I would stop and be silent and listen to God.

I use Scripture to stimulate my prayer life. Reading a psalm and turning it into a prayer is very enriching. A friend of mine says that when we pray the Psalms, we are praying in union with Jesus who hallowed the Psalms by his own use of them.

The verse 'pray without ceasing' is an invitation to pray at any time and in any place. I find I can pray when I am standing in a queue and see the unhappy face of someone who looks burdened. I often pray for my neighbours as I walk down my street and breathe the prayer over every front door: 'peace be to this house'. If I am commanded to love my neighbour, the practice of loving them begins with prayer.

Finally, praying with others is a great encouragement. Prayer groups reveal those with the gift of faith and the ministry of intercession. Praying with others doesn't unlock all of our closed doors, but it does release deep wisdom and prophetic insight and it builds a persevering faith.

LYNDON BOWRING
Chairman, Care

For years I felt guilty about not praying enough. But God has helped me to inject some old-fashioned *daily drill* into my prayer life, which works for me.

I always carry a card listing a whole bunch of people I pray for. So, whether I'm walking, travelling, at my desk or in my favourite 'prayer chair', I refer daily to it.

This is often a chore but the *thrill* of completing the list gives me such a sense of accomplishment, and it's a real guilt-buster!

I also pray Matthew 5:8, *'purify my heart'* or *'purify my motives'*, so I can more clearly 'see' God at work.

I pray the Lord's Prayer daily, pausing particularly on 'Your will be done' – *'show me Your desires today'* and 'Lead me not into temptation' – *'help me to humble myself and not need to be led into temptation'*.

And almost always, *the thrill outweighs the drill!*

GRAHAM KENDRICK
**Singer-songwriter and Co-founder of
March for Jesus**

'Choose your rut carefully – you'll be in it for a hundred miles!' So reads the graffiti on a sign at the beginning of a remote Australian outback road. Prayer can develop its ruts as well, especially if our topics and language are determined mostly by our felt needs, ingrained habits or prevailing mood.

Although it is better to pray in a rut than not pray at all, the Bible has a built-in escape device. It is called the Psalms. When I use these Holy Spirit-inspired heart-cries as a preparation for prayer – ideally read out loud – I take God's prayer agenda, His nuggets of truth, divine perspectives, phrases and praises on my lips, and my eyes are raised to the greatness of the God who answers prayer. Spontaneity is great – when it happens! But the Psalms are God's elevator to lift our own prayers to another level entirely.

NATIONAL DISTRIBUTORS

UK: (and countries not listed below)
CWR, Waverley Abbey House, Waverley Lane, Farnham, Surrey GU9 8EP.
Tel: (01252) 784700 Outside UK +44 1252 784700

AUSTRALIA: CMC Australasia, PO Box 519, Belmont, Victoria 3216.
Tel: (03) 5241 3288 Fax: (03) 5241 3290

CANADA: Cook Communications Ministries, PO Box 98, 55 Woodslee Avenue,
Paris, Ontario N3L 3E5. Tel: 1800 263 2664

GHANA: Challenge Enterprises of Ghana, PO Box 5723, Accra.
Tel: (021) 222437/223249 Fax: (021) 226227

HONG KONG: Cross Communications Ltd, 1/F, 562A Nathan Road, Kowloon.
Tel: 2780 1188 Fax: 2770 6229

INDIA: Crystal Communications, 10-3-18/4/1, East Marredpalli, Secunderabad
– 500026, Andhra Pradesh Tel/Fax: (040) 27737145

KENYA: Keswick Books and Gifts Ltd, PO Box 10242, Nairobi.
Tel: (02) 331692/226047 Fax: (02) 728557

MALAYSIA: Salvation Book Centre (M) Sdn Bhd, 23 Jalan SS 2/64, 47300
Petaling Jaya, Selangor. Tel: (03) 78766411/78766797 Fax: (03) 78757066/78756360

NEW ZEALAND: CMC Australasia, PO Box 36015, Lower Hutt.
Tel: 0800 449 408 Fax: 0800 449 049

NIGERIA: FBFM, Helen Baugh House, 96 St Finbarr's College Road, Akoka, Lagos.
Tel: (01) 7747429/4700218/825775/827264

PHILIPPINES: OMF Literature Inc, 776 Boni Avenue, Mandaluyong City.
Tel: (02) 531 2183 Fax: (02) 531 1960

SOUTH AFRICA: Struik Christian Books, 80 MacKenzie Street, PO Box 1144,
Cape Town 8000. Tel: (021) 462 4360 Fax: (021) 461 3612

SRI LANKA: Christombu Publications (Pvt) Ltd., Bartleet House, 65 Braybrooke
Place, Colombo 2. Tel: (9411) 2421073/2447665

TANZANIA: CLC Christian Book Centre, PO Box 1384, Mkwepu Street,
Dar es Salaam. Tel/Fax: (022) 2119439

USA: Cook Communications Ministries, PO Box 98, 55 Woodslee Avenue, Paris,
Ontario N3L 3E5, Canada. Tel: 1800 263 2664

ZIMBABWE: Word of Life Books (Pvt) Ltd, Christian Media Centre, 8 Aberdeen
Road, Avondale, PO Box A480 Avondale, Harare. Tel: (04) 333355 or 091301188

For email addresses, visit the CWR website: www.cwr.org.uk
CWR is a registered charity – Number 294387
CWR is a limited company registered in England – Registration
Number 1990308

PRAYER – A FRESH VISION
Selwyn Hughes

This book encourages us to take a fresh look at our prayer life, and teaches us how to offer effective prayers that touch the heart of God and keep us in His will. Don't miss talking with your Father in heaven; learn the essentials of effective prayer; and know more about worship, adoration, thanksgiving and praise.

£6.99 (plus p & p)

ISBN-13: 978-1-85345-308-3
ISBN-10: 1-85345-308-0
Price correct at time of going to print.

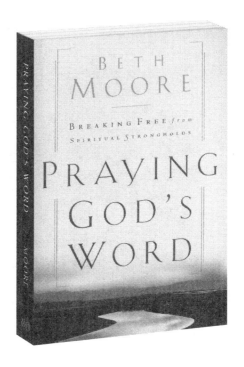

PRAYING GOD'S WORD
Beth Moore

A topical prayer guide, addressing fourteen common strongholds and what Scripture reveals about each of them. *Praying God's Word* presents Scripture in prayer form to be incorporated into our daily prayer life. God's word, through prayer, helps us overcome bitterness, anger and unforgiveness and sets us free.

£7.99 (plus p & p)
ISBN-13: 978-1-85345-360-1
ISBN-10: 1-85345-360-9
Price correct at time of going to print.

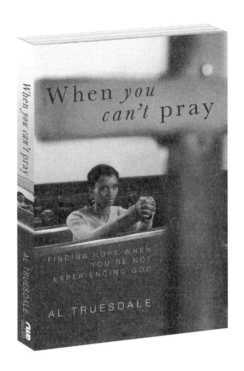

WHEN YOU CAN'T PRAY
Al Truesdale

When You Can't Pray is written for those whose prayer life has broken down and feels meaningless. The author probes difficulties and frustrations of the Christian walk, such as life's tragedies and profound doubt. Al Truesdale brings you full circle from doubt and disappointment to God's unconditional love for you.

£7.99 (plus p & p)

ISBN-13: 978-1-85345-349-6
ISBN-10: 1-85345-349-8
Price correct at time of going to print.